Mary's Christmas

Angela Q. Bertone

Edited by Emily T. Mayeaux, B.A., M.Ed.

Illustrated by Ariane O'Pry

ISBN: 0615692834

ISBN-13: 978-0615692838

Library of Congress Control Number: 2012916416

Ask Angela Productions, Ponchatoula, Louisiana

Dedication

I dedicate this book to my mother, Sarah Lou Lea Quezada. Before my mother passed, she asked me to write some things for her. This book is an answer to one of her last requests. The heart of my mom shall live on in the joy of storytelling that she nurtured in me. I love you, Mom, and I trust you are pleased with the story you left in my soul to share with the world.

Acknowledgments

With a grateful heart I say thank you to Michael Bertone, Sr. You are my best friend, a wonderful father and the husband I prayed for.

You believe in me when I can't believe in myself, encourage me when I put my dreams on the shelf, challenge me when my work is not the best it can be and rejoice with me in seeing my dreams come true.

Thank you, honey, for all that you have done and all that you do to encourage and support me.

Words can't express what I feel in my heart for you, so I will spend my life showing you.

Mary's Christmas

It was a cold night in Bethlehem during lambing season, and one of the ewes on Joachim's small farm was in deep trouble. Triplets were not common and delivering them was very dangerous for both the ewe and the lambs.

Mary, Joachim's young daughter, watched from the shadows as he assisted the mother. All three lambs were delivered alive, but the littlest one did not look like it would survive. The mother ewe had rejected it, and Joachim was just about to put the little lamb down. He knew that it was more humane to end its life than to let it suffer.

Surprising her father, Mary leapt from her hiding place and yelled, "Stop! Please, Daddy, no. Let it live."

Joachim turned to Mary and knelt down for her to see the little lamb. It looked absolutely perfect. Its wool was the whitest she had ever seen. Not one spot marked it.

"I beg you, Dad. Please let me take care of it."

Joachim sighed. "That's too much work, Mary. You will have to care for it night and day. And what about your chores?"

"I can do it. I will sleep out here in the barn every night, and I can make a bed for him right here in this manger. I will do all of my chores too, I promise."

Reluctantly, her father agreed. He could not resist her compassionate heart. Besides, he knew the lamb wouldn't last three days, and then Mary could get back to her normal routine.

Mary looked up into heaven and prayed, *Oh Father, please don't let him die.*

Just then, a star in the eastern sky began to glow more brilliantly than any star she had ever seen. As the barnyard grew brighter, a calm fell over the animals. Mary had never known such a silent night. Maybe it was a sign the lamb would live, she thought.

Mary's mother, Anne, helped prepare the barn for the rough days ahead. The first three were difficult, but Mary kept all of her promises. Her father was amazed and commended Mary for her efforts when he realized the lamb would live after all.

Mary had become the little lamb's mother, and he followed her everywhere she went. Mary named him Starlight, after the miracle star that lit up the sky the night he was born.

Months went by, and soon Passover was only a few days off. Joachim hired a young man named Joseph to help him load the animals. Preparation for the holy day was lots of work and everyone was very busy, including Mary.

Joachim approached Mary and said gently, "Mary, it's time."

"Time for what, Dad?"

"Time to take the animals to Jerusalem."

Mary nodded. "Yes, Dad, I will have everything ready in time to leave."

"No, Mary, you don't understand . . . it's Starlight."

"What about Starlight?" Mary asked.

"He must go too."

"Go where?"

Joachim put his hand on her shoulder. "To market."

"For what?"

"Mary, you know. He is the best lamb on this farm. He's spotless. He could bring 30 pieces. Do you know how much money that is?"

Mary held Starlight tight and began to cry. "But, Daddy, he is mine. You were going to kill him, and I saved him. Please … don't take him to die," she begged.

"I have no choice," Joachim said softly. "Passover requires a spotless lamb, and we must give our very best to God."

Sobbing, Mary carried Starlight to the wagon and climbed in. She held him close. "If he must go, then I will ride in here with him," she said.

As they rode to Jerusalem, Mary prayed without stopping. *Why must the innocent die?* she asked God.

Just then, Mary heard a voice.

"I wanted to be like the promised Messiah, so our Father sent me to you," the voice began. "Some animals sacrifice milk, some eggs, and some meat. I came to give my life. I needed you to save me so I could save the people.

One day, God will send his son to save the world and no more animals will have to die for sin. I am a lamb of God, but he shall be 'The Lamb of God'. He will bring peace on Earth and goodwill toward men. They shall call the day of his birth Christmas and rejoice. When you cry for me, remember that I wanted to be like the Son of God."

Mary pondered these things in her heart. "I'll never forget you, Starlight. I will sing songs about you and how you followed me everywhere, and about the twinkling star."

Tears of joy and sadness streamed down her face as the wagon continued toward the holy city.

Mary did not know it yet, but God would soon use her to send Jesus–who would be born in a stable and laid in a manger under a starlit sky where angels would declare peace on Earth and goodwill toward men.

Postscript

To all the moms and dads, aunts and uncles, teachers and leaders: Thank you for taking the time to share this book with your loved ones. I trust you know and understand that this book is in no way intended to add to the scriptures of our Lord and Savior Jesus.

In response to my mother's dying request I wrote this book, and I hope I have brought honor to my mother and to the mother of Jesus. I am sure we could never imagine what she went through in being chosen as the mother of God, but I do pray as I release future fiction stories of Mary's life, that you as my reader will appreciate my efforts and imagine with me what her life may have looked like.

This Christian fiction is intended for our enjoyment and encouragement. I hope this book can and will be used to assist us and our loved ones in understanding how life often brings us through difficult times, and to remind us that the testing of our faith produces endurance. The Bible tells us that we should let endurance have *its* perfect result, so that we may be perfect and complete, lacking in nothing. We can also be assured that God will use each test we face to strengthen our hearts and better prepare us for whatever trials may lie in the future.

Let us all be aware, this life comes with no guarantees. However, Jesus promised to be with us even until the end.

About the Author

Angela Q. Bertone was born and raised in Livingston, Louisiana, and is one of six children. She gives honor to her mother, and credits her with passing down the art of storytelling. She finds joy in remembering her mother's gift for crafting her own original stories, as well as for bringing the tales of others to life by providing each character with a unique voice. One of Angela's childhood favorites is the tale of Br'er Fox and Br'er Rabbit, from a full-color, illustrated hardback version of Joel Chandler Harris's *Uncle Remus*.

Angela followed in her mother's footsteps and often performed "dinner theater" with her children. She dressed herself and her children as different story characters while they shared lunch and watched movies. She even spoke in character as she served her children, hoping to pass on her mother's traditions and her enthusiasm for storytelling.

Today, Angela is fulfilling her dream of becoming a published author. Her first book is a self-published spiritual/inspirational work called *Good Mourning Sunshine*. Read more about Angela and her writing on her website, www.angelabertone.com

Look for the Easter-themed sequel to *Mary's Christmas,* scheduled for release in March 2013.

www.ingramcontent.com/pod-product-compliance
Lightning Source LLC
Chambersburg PA
CBHW041550040426
42447CB00002B/130

* 9 7 8 0 6 1 5 6 9 2 8 3 8 *